THE
SIOUX

Peter Hicks

Wayland

Look into the Past

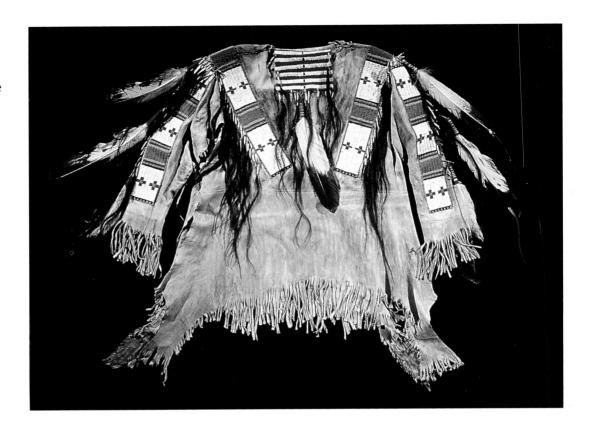

Series editor: Joanna Bentley
Series designer: David West
Book designer: Joyce Chester

First published in 1994 by Wayland (Publishers) Limited,
61 Western Road, Hove, East Sussex, BN3 1JD, England

© Copyright 1994 Wayland (Publishers) Limited

British Library Cataloguing in Publication Data
Hicks, Peter
Sioux. – (Look into the Past series)
I. Title II. Series
978.00497

ISBN 0 7502 1069 9

Typeset by Dorchester Typesetting Group Ltd., Dorset,
England.
Printed and bound in Italy by L.E.G.O. S.p.A., Vicenza.

Picture acknowledgements
The publishers wish to thank the following for providing the
photographs in this book: Archiv für Kunst und Geschichte,
Berlin 23 (bottom); Werner Forman Archive *cover*, 4, 5
(top, Robinson Museum, South Dakota, USA), 6 (Museum
für Volkerkunde, Berlin), 7 (all, Plains Indian Museum,
Cody, Wyoming, USA), 8 (top, Robinson Museum, bottom
Plains Indian Museum), 9 (bottom, Museum of the
American Indian, New York), 10, 13 (top, Glenbow
Museum, Calgary, USA), 14 (Plains Indian Museum), 16
(right, Plains Indian Museum), 17 (top, Plains Indian
Museum), 20 (both Plains Indian Museum) 22 (left, Museum
für Volkerkunde, Berlin), 23 (top, Field Museum of Natural
History, Chicago), 24 (British Museum); Peter Newark's
Western Americana 5 (bottom), 11 (top), 16 (left), 18, 22
(right), 25 (top), 26; Colin Taylor *cover*, 9 (top), 11
(bottom), 12 (top and bottom/middle), 15 (both), 17
(bottom), 19 (both), 21 (bottom), 27 (both), 28, 29.
Map artwork by Jenny Hughes.

CONTENTS

Words that appear in **bold italic** in the text are explained in the glossary on page 30.

WHO ARE THE SIOUX?

The Sioux, or Dakota Indians to give them their proper name, are a North American Plains tribe that descended from the *migrants* who came to America from Asia 30,000 years ago. The name Sioux is actually an insult meaning 'snake', given to them by an enemy tribe.

As you can see from the map, the Sioux first ▶ came from just west of the Great Lakes, but most were pushed westwards by other tribes into South Dakota. The Eastern, or Sante Sioux and the Middle, or Nakota Sioux, were both hunter-gatherers and farmers. In this book we are going to concentrate on the Western or Lakota Sioux, who were hunter-gatherers and led a *nomadic* life style. Many tribes including the Lakota Sioux, trekked across the plains searching for the animal they depended upon – the bison.

◀ The plains of North America are a huge expanse of grassland that stretches from Texas in the south to Canada in the north. There are some tree-covered hills and mountains, and rocky outcrops, but the plains are largely flat, as you can see in the photograph.

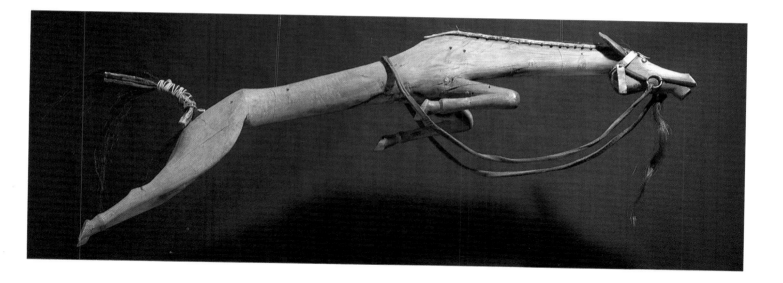

▲ Until the 1600s the Sioux hunted on foot. However, by about 1650 the life of these nomads had changed dramatically. The horse, introduced by the Spanish in South America, reached the Plains tribes. On horseback, the Lakota could hunt bison faster and farther afield. This remarkable model shows the power and speed of a war pony. Here was another use of the horse: war parties could swiftly attack neighbouring tribes, take them by surprise and steal their prized possessions – mainly horses!

◀ Because the Lakota were often on the move, they developed a special type of house – the tipi. When the tribe broke camp, the tipi, with its soft hide covering stretched over wooden poles, could be taken down very quickly. The poles made up the *travois* on to which the rolled-up hides and other possessions were fastened. In the photograph look at the construction of the tipi. The gap at the top is for smoke from the fire.

5

THE TRIBE AND ITS WAYS

The Lakota Sioux were such a large tribe that they divided up into seven separate bands. The most powerful was the Oglala, which produced such fine and famous warriors as Red Cloud and Crazy Horse. The Lakota's movements depended on the bison. In spring and summer many bands joined up to follow the huge grazing herds and kill enough meat for their needs. As well as meat they ate wild fruits and vegetables, such as cherries, potatoes, onions and turnips. These were gathered during autumn and stored for the long, harsh winter, which was usually spent camped in sheltered river valleys.

▼ We have already seen that a nomadic life style made the portable tipi essential. Cooking utensils and containers were also portable. Pottery was useless as it was heavy and likely to break. Most vessels were made of hide, such as the parfleche in the picture. This was a piece of hide that folded like an envelope and was used to carry dried meat and other foods. These highly decorated and prized objects were often presented as gifts. They could be used as saddle-bags or inside the tipi.

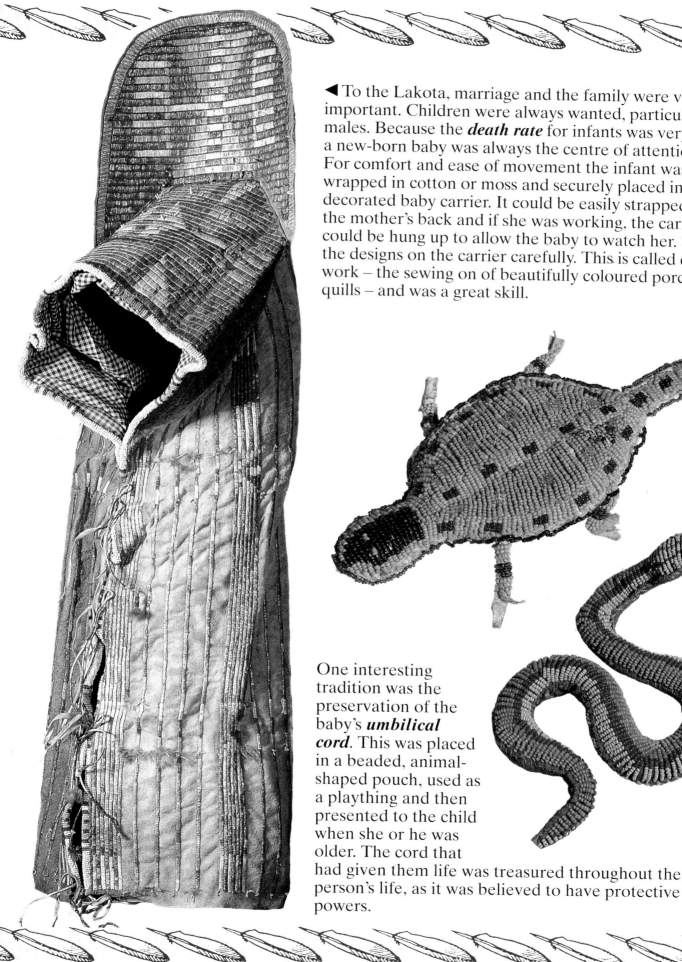

◄ To the Lakota, marriage and the family were very important. Children were always wanted, particularly males. Because the **death rate** for infants was very high, a new-born baby was always the centre of attention. For comfort and ease of movement the infant was wrapped in cotton or moss and securely placed inside a decorated baby carrier. It could be easily strapped to the mother's back and if she was working, the carrier could be hung up to allow the baby to watch her. Study the designs on the carrier carefully. This is called quill-work – the sewing on of beautifully coloured porcupine quills – and was a great skill.

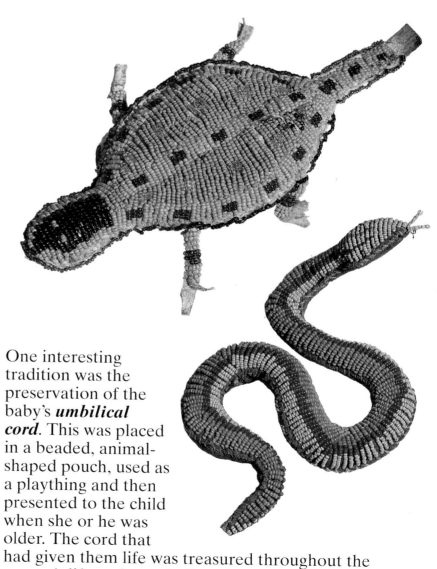

One interesting tradition was the preservation of the baby's **umbilical cord**. This was placed in a beaded, animal-shaped pouch, used as a plaything and then presented to the child when she or he was older. The cord that had given them life was treasured throughout the person's life, as it was believed to have protective powers.

7

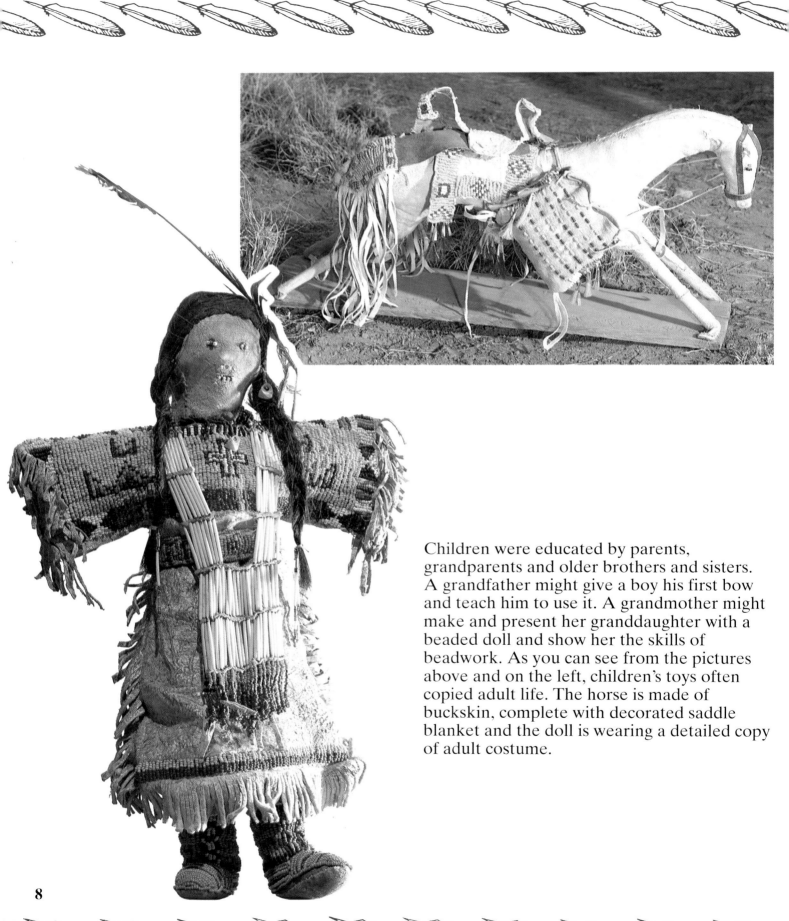

Children were educated by parents, grandparents and older brothers and sisters. A grandfather might give a boy his first bow and teach him to use it. A grandmother might make and present her granddaughter with a beaded doll and show her the skills of beadwork. As you can see from the pictures above and on the left, children's toys often copied adult life. The horse is made of buckskin, complete with decorated saddle blanket and the doll is wearing a detailed copy of adult costume.

8

One *ritual* amongst Sioux men was the smoking of pipes. This was rarely done for pleasure, but on occasions of great importance, such as a guest's first visit to the tipi or the final agreement on a friendship or deal. The picture shows a pipe and tobacco bag with quill embroidery and a fringe. ▶

Gifts of pipes or tobacco were highly prized. The wooden stem was often decorated with quills, while the bowl was usually made of a soft stone called pipestone. This special pipe bowl is made of slate. Notice the superbly carved couple and horse's head. ▼

9

BISON!

Before the introduction of horses to the plains, the Lakota hunted bison on foot. This was very difficult because of the dangers of large herds running at speed. Using disguises, such as wolf skins, the hunters had to approach the herd downwind, for the bison has a very good sense of smell. On these bison hunts the Sioux managed to kill large numbers of animals in very clever ways.

◄ In winter the hunters drove bison into deep snow-drifts and killed them. Also, large numbers were **stampeded** over cliffs like the one in the photograph. In these stampedes, known as the piskun, the bison were either killed outright, or those that were injured were picked off at the foot of the cliff. This site has been *excavated* by *archaeologists* and bison remains and arrowheads dating from AD 600 have been found.

▲ Once the horse reached the Lakota, it was possible to kill larger numbers of bison. The mounted hunters charged into the herd, causing a stampede, and were joined by others riding alongside firing arrows and hurling spears. The bison hunt, with its noise, dust and confusion, was still very dangerous as you can see from the painting. Both horse and rider were in constant danger, for a bull could weigh up to 1,000 kilos!

Hunters brought down the number of bison ▼ required. With specially strengthened bows only used on these hunts, stone or iron-tipped arrows were fired with great force into the shoulders, necks and sides of the running bison. The power of these bows, often lovingly decorated, was proved by their use long after the introduction of the gun. Their small size – less than one metre long – made them easy to handle, even while riding a pony at full speed.

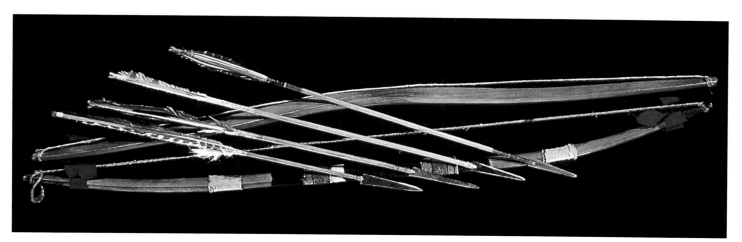

▲ Look carefully at this scene. Who is taking part in the **butchering** of the dead bison? The butchering was carried out with great enthusiasm, for the tribe had secured food for the future. The cut meat would be loaded on to travois and taken to camp. There the best meat might be given to the tribal leaders and other members who helped in the hunt. The rest was either eaten or cut into strips, dried and pounded – called **pemmican** – so it would keep for months.

Can you see the woman preparing the pemmican in the bottom left of this picture? Of course, the bison was not used only for food. The hide was very important and had to be specially treated. First the fur and inside fat and tissue had to be scraped off with sharp stones. Then it was stretched and twisted many times before it could be made into items such as tipi covers, belts, shields, **moccasins**, shirts and bedcovers. ▶

▲ The rest of the bison *carcass* provided the tribe with many of its raw materials. For example, sinew, the tissue that connects muscle to the bone, made bow strings and thread. Horns were shaped into cups and spoons. Bones were used for knives, saddle frames and shovels (from the shoulder-blades). Clearly, the bison was essential for the Lakota and they honoured it constantly. If the herds ever disappeared, for whatever reason, disaster would strike. **13**

APPEARANCE

Lakota clothing was fairly simple and, with the harsh winters and hot summers of the plains, it varied according to season. In summer, for example, both men and women usually wore lighter deer or elk skin and, because of the heat, *tattooing* and personal ornaments replaced a lot of clothing.

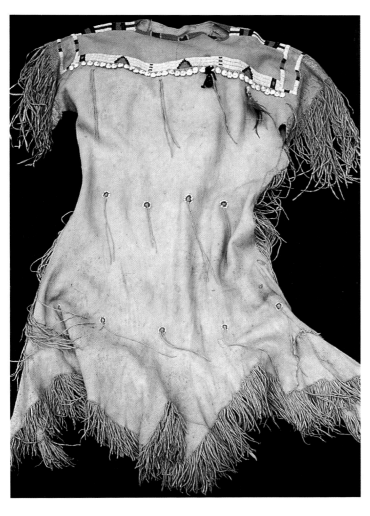

◀ Women wore soft skin dresses, over knee-length leggings. Look at the dress in the picture. Notice the highly decorated yoke at the top and the attractive fringes on the arms and hem. The yoke was usually made of elks' teeth, shells and beads.

These women's leggings, with attractive *geometric* quill designs, would have kept the wearer warm in the winter. Men's leggings were ankle-length and loose for comfort on horseback, with a beaded strip up either side. ▼

◀ The most important item of clothing was the bison robe. Robes made from the hide of young female bisons were highly prized. For winter wear, the hair was left on, but summer robes were scraped to make them thinner and lighter. Study this robe carefully. Is it for winter or summer use? Can you work out the head and legs of the animal? How do you think it was worn?

15

Both men and women wore their hair in two braids – or plaits – one at either side of the head. The braids were often decorated with colourful cloth, fur or beads and this showed the status of the wearer. Look at the photograph of Red Shirt, a member of Sitting Bull's Hunkpapa band. Although he is wearing the waistcoat and shirt of the white man, notice the braided hair and decoration. Around his neck he is wearing the traditional shell choker and holding his pipe and tobacco pouch. ▼

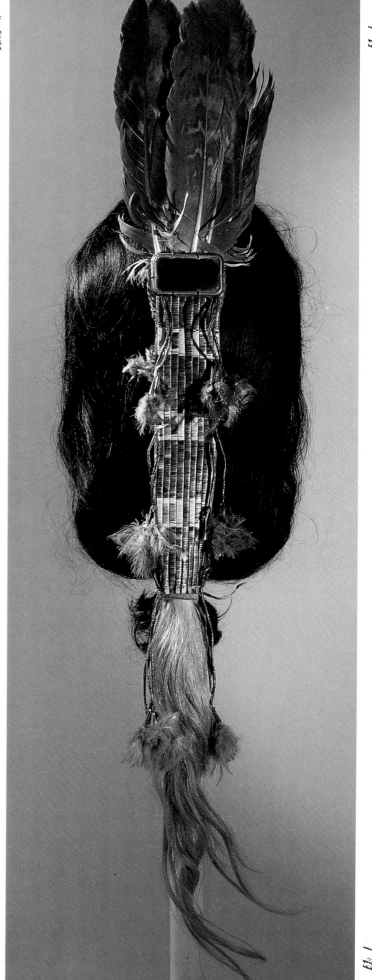

◀ The back of the head was also decorated. This wonderful quill and feather hair ornament dates from about 1890. Can you see how the feathers are kept in place? A mirror plate has been used. Similar mirrors were used to make signals in the wars with the US army. The number of feathers was a mark of the man's war achievements.

The Lakota were ▶ justly proud of their colourful appearance. These armbands, beautifully decorated with quills and feathers, were probably worn during the many ceremonial dances that were held at various times of the year.

◀ Footwear consisted of the famous moccasins. They were tough and comfortable – the soles were made of hard, untanned bison skin, and the uppers from softer, *tanned* hide. As you can see, they were often lavishly decorated with colourful beads, sewn all around.

17

WARRIOR!

By the nineteenth century the Lakota were a powerful military force. Their warriors on horseback took more land and forced weaker farming tribes to provide them with food. With horse stealing being the main activity between tribes (horses meant wealth), the Lakota made enemies – particularly the Crow and Pawnee who bordered on their territory. We know that bows and arrows were important, but what other weapons were used in these raids?

A traditional ▶ weapon was the war club. This was a polished, pointed stone head, with a long wooden handle. Bison rawhide always shrinks and this kept the head permanently in place. The long handle would give a mounted warrior a long reach during a fight.

The early guns brought by white traders were not much use to the mounted warriors because they were so difficult to load. However, as guns improved, so warriors were keen to own them. The photograph shows a single-shot Springfield Carbine of 1873 used by the Lakota. With the coming of the repeating rifles, which did not need frequent reloading, they became even more effective *cavalrymen*. ▶

Shields were very ▶ important for many reasons. A well-made, round rawhide shield, perhaps padded with bison hair, could stop a swift arrow or an old-fashioned *musket* ball. Shields were decorated with magical paintings, showing powerful animals such as eagles or grizzly bears. The power of these animals was thought to pass to the shield's owner. Some warriors were so sure of their powers that they rode into battle with only the shield for cover!

◄ A brave and skilful warrior was recognized in a number of ways. The eagle feather war bonnet (above and left) was a sign of a great fighter. The bonnet was cleverly made so that when its owner walked, the feathers moved like the eagle in flight – graceful and silent. The size of the bonnet often showed the greatness of a warrior. The feather part of this bonnet is called a trailer and each eagle feather represents an act of bravery in battle. Clearly, these bonnets were only worn by the most outstanding fighters.

▲ Another sign of a good fighter was the war shirt. Beautifully made in soft deerskin, the proud wearer would display signs of bravery. Can you see the feathers and hair fringes attached to the front and shoulders? These represented coups (see below), or even the scalps of enemies. Scalping – the removal of the top of an enemy's head and hair – was a sign of total victory. Afterwards you 'owned' your enemy, because a person's spirit was thought to be in the hair.

◀ An unusual honour in battle was the counting coup. It was considered very brave to ride or run up to an armed enemy and strike him on the head, shoulder or arm. This would be done with the hand or a special stick. You can see this taking place in the picture. If the blow had been witnessed, the successful warrior gained great honour. To have a count coup against you was considered shameful. Look again at the man striking the blow. How can you tell he is a great warrior?

RELIGION AND BELIEFS

Lakota religion was based on all things 'wakan' or sacred. Everything in the world came from Wakan Tanka – the Great Spirit, Mystery or Medicine. After death people would join Wakan Tanka in the afterlife. On Earth he communicated with chosen men, called Shaman (which means holy men), who are sometimes called medicine men. They were obviously very important people in the band. Beneath the Great Spirit were four more gods – the Earth, Rock, Sun and Sky. Beneath these were the lower gods: the Bison, Bear, Four Winds and Whirlwind.

▲ The Shaman was not only the go-between for the band and the Great Spirit, but he also had to cure illness. He knew herbal remedies for everyday problems like headaches and toothaches. Serious illnesses were more difficult and he had to receive help from sacred animals like the eagle. This is a shaman's eagle-wing fan, which he used when treating sick people.

▲ The Shaman also helped to organize the most important event of the Lakota year – the Sun Dance. Many bands came together, bringing thousands of members for feasting and festivity. The purpose of the dance was to ensure a plentiful supply of bison. If it did not take place the herds would disappear and the plants would die. Those chosen for the dance had to offer up pain and suffering, as you can see in the picture. From a central pole came two ropes and they were attached to the dancer's chest. The dancer pulled against the ropes until finally ripping free. The noise from drums and whistles going on for many days made it a dramatic ceremony.

There were many other dances celebrating various events and these were also opportunities for dressing up. The Night Dance, when partners chose each other, was a great social occasion. The Scalp Dance celebrated victories in battle and the newly won scalps were displayed.

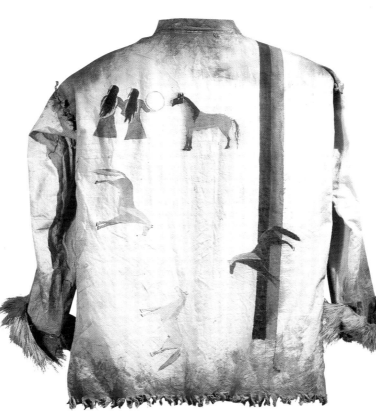

◀ Both the beat of drums and singing were central to these ceremonies. Because of their importance the bison and horse figured in many dances. The power of the horse is celebrated on this beautifully painted shirt worn during the 'grass in the belt dance' or Grass Dance.

▲ Among the Lakota, death was taken seriously, but not usually feared by old people. If a child died, relatives would mourn by cutting their flesh and hair and ripping clothing. When a person died the body was usually wrapped with personal objects and placed on a *scaffold* outside the village or in a tree. These burial places were visited and it was known for older widows to wear the jaw-bone of their dead husband.

WAR AND DEFEAT

During the 1860s the Lakota, led by Red Cloud, went to war with the *white man*. They hated the roads and forts built on their land by the US army to protect gold miners travelling to the Rockies. Red Cloud's war was successful – the government in Washington withdrew the army because of the cost. After the Lakota burnt down all the forts a *treaty* was signed. The government agreed to a Great Sioux Reservation – land reserved for the Sioux 'as long as the grass shall grow'.

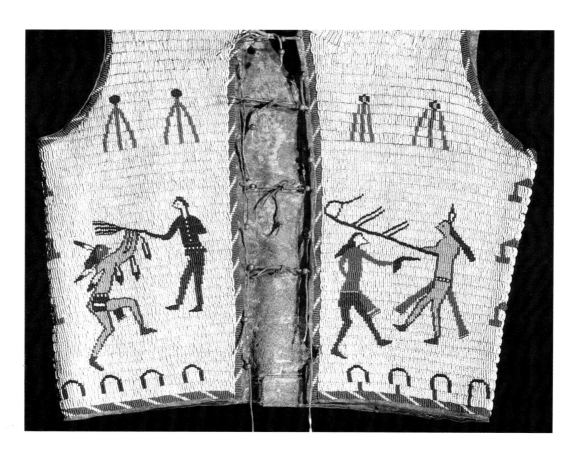

However, by 1874 there were stories that there was gold in the Black Hills – part of the Reservation and very sacred land. Although whites were not allowed on the Black Hills a gold rush started and thousands of miners flocked into the area. The Lakota obviously attacked them, to defend their homeland. Soon the army was sent in to protect the miners. This beaded jacket shows scenes from the fighting.

The Lakota were ▶ so concerned about this threat that they joined up with another tribe, the Cheyenne. The government offered the Lakota $6 million for the Black Hills but this was rejected. War was sure to follow. The main Lakota chief and Shaman, Sitting Bull, whom you can see in the picture, had a great vision that many white men would fall into their camp and be killed.

The Lakota and Cheyenne formed a large camp near the Big Horn River during June 1876. The army hoped to encircle this camp and destroy it. General Custer, with over 600 men, decided to attack without waiting for support. However, Custer and a close group of about 200 soldiers became surrounded by bands of Oglala, Hunkpapa and Cheyenne. Within one hour Custer and his men were all dead. ▼

Despite this great Sioux victory, the US government was determined to break the power of the Lakota and put them all on reservations. Crazy Horse kept attacking the miners but when he gave himself up in 1877 he was murdered by the army. The reservations were on the poorest land, yet the whites expected the Sioux to farm. More importantly, the government allowed white hunters to destroy the great bison herds. This meant the animal the Sioux most needed for clothing, shelter and food was disappearing. This was done deliberately to make the Lakota dependent on money from the US authorities. ▼

Not surprisingly, the Lakota hated this life. They were used to a free life, following the bison. By 1890 a strange ceremony swept through the Plains, called the Ghost Dance. The dancers clothed themselves in special shirts and robes and entered a *trance*. By dancing, they believed the bison would return and the white men leave. The army was called in to stamp it out. In one skirmish Sitting Bull was murdered. ▶

Another Lakota chief, Big Foot, wanted by ▶ the army for allowing the Ghost Dance, tried to reach the safety of Red Cloud's reservation. He and over 300 Lakota were arrested in December 1890 at Wounded Knee. In a scuffle over a gun the army fired on the band killing nearly all the men, women and children. Big Foot and the other bodies were left out to freeze in the snow. The Lakota never recovered from this *massacre*.

THE SIOUX TODAY

The hundred years since Wounded Knee have been very hard for the Sioux population. They have survived, but at a great cost. For example, early Sioux schools took young children away from their families and tried to make them think and act like whites. They were not allowed to speak their own language or follow the old beliefs. Over the years, native Americans have become the poorest *ethnic minority* in America. In 1985 there were over 54,000 Sioux living on reservations in South Dakota alone. What are conditions like?

Unfortunately, much reservation housing is poor. Wooden cabins like this one at Standing Rock rarely have hot and cold running water, electricity or **sanitation.** Poor housing often leads to poor health, and native Americans have high rates of diseases such as tuberculosis, diabetes and dysentry. The infant death rate is high and native Americans die much younger than whites. Unemployment is high on the reservations and many Sioux have moved to towns to look for work. Some people feel trapped between the familiar reservation and the unfamiliar towns and cities.

◀ A large number of Sioux make a living out of the tourist industry – many white people are very interested in native American culture. This display of Sioux costume is in the Buffalo Bill Historical Center in Wyoming, USA.

Many Sioux feel that things will only get better if education improves. Since 1975 a law has allowed tribes to run their own schools and provide, very importantly, a Sioux *curriculum*. In this way, they can celebrate and protect their history and culture, and at the same time come to terms with the modern world. These modern tipis show that native American traditions have carried on in some areas over the years.

GLOSSARY

Archaeologists   People who study objects and remains from ancient times.

Butchering   Cutting up an animal into pieces that can be used as meat to eat.

Carcass   The dead body of an animal.

Cavalrymen   Soldiers who fight on horseback.

Curriculum   A course of study at school or college.

Death rate   The number of deaths in a particular area or age range.

Ethnic minority   A group of people of one race, living in a country where most people are of another race.

Excavated   To have dug up buried remains.

Geometric   A pattern made up of regular shapes.

Massacre   Savage killing of large numbers of people.

Migrants   People who move from one country or part of the world to another.

Moccasins   Shoes made from soft leather.

Musket   A long-barrelled gun that fired single lead balls.

Nomadic   Describing nomads, people who do not have fixed homes, but move from place to place.

Pemmican   A small pressed cake of shredded, dried meat, pounded into paste with fat and berries.

Pictograph   A picture or symbol standing for a word or group of words.

Ritual   A set way of performing a ceremony.

Sanitation   The use of proper cleaning arrangements to protect health.

Scaffold   A raised wooden platform.

Stampeded   Scared a herd of animals into running in one direction.

Tanned   Treated animal hide to turn it into leather.

Tattooing   Making designs or pictures on the skin by pricking it and staining it with colour.

Trance   A sleeplike state.

Travois   A type of sled made with two poles in a frame that was pulled by an animal.

Treaty   A formal agreement between two or more states or countries.

Umbilical cord   The long cord that connects a baby to its mother before it is born.

White man   The men who ruled the USA were white settlers.

IMPORTANT DATES

c 30,000 BC First migrants reach North America from Asia

up to 1400s AD Sioux settle in the headwaters of the Mississippi

1500s Sioux migrate to plains after war with the Cree

1519 The Spanish, led by Cortes, introduce the horse to America

1600s The horse reaches the plains

1841 First wagon trains trek across the plains

1866 Red Cloud's war against the US army begins

1868 Red Cloud signs Laramie Treaty
Huge Lakota reservation set up

1874 Gold rush to the Black Hills on the Lakota reservation, bringing in thousands of white miners

1875 Lakota and Cheyenne join forces for Summer Sun Dance

1876 US army campaign against Lakota and Cheyenne begins
Lakota and Cheyenne victory at the Battle of Little Bighorn
General Custer killed

1877 Lakota surrender to US army. They lose Powder River County and the Black Hills
September: Crazy Horse murdered

1889 Break up of the Great Lakota reservation

1890 October-November: Ghost Dance sweeps the plains
December: Sitting Bull murdered, Massacre at Wounded Knee

BOOKS TO READ

Plains Indians by Anne Smith (Wayland, 1989).
This book will tell you about the Plains Indians of yesterday and how they live today.

Learning about the Plains Indians by C. Taylor (Simon & Shuster, 1993).
This book looks at the lifestyles of different Plains Indian tribes.

INDEX